Animals and the Environment
Snakes

Coral Snakes

by Linda George

Content Consultant:
Donal M. Boyer
Associate Curator
Reptile Department
San Diego Zoo

CAPSTONE BOOKS
an imprint of Capstone Press
Mankato, Minnesota

Capstone Books are published by Capstone Press
151 Good Counsel Drive, P.O. Box 669, Mankato, Minnesota 56002
http://www.capstone-press.com

Library of Congress Cataloging-in-Publication Data
George, Linda.
 Coral snakes/by Linda George.
   p. cm.--(Animals and the environment)
 Includes bibliographical references (p. 44) and index.
 Summary: Describes the physical characteristics, habitat, and behavior of coral snakes.
 ISBN 1-56065-692-1
   1. Coral snakes--Juvenile literature. [1. Coral snakes. 2. Poisonous snakes. 3. Snakes.] I. Title. II. Series: Animals & the environment.
QL666.O64G465 1998
597.96--dc21

                                          97-31673
                                            CIP
                                            AC

Editorial credits:
Editor, Matt Doeden; cover design, Timothy Halldin; illustrations, James Franklin; photo research, Michelle L. Norstad

Photo credits:
Michael Cardwell and Associates, 8, 13 (top), 18, 21, 30
Suzanne L. Collins & Joseph T. Collins, 29
Dembinsky Photo Assoc. Inc./Allen Blake Sheldon, 40
KAC Productions/John & Gloria Tventen, 36
Bill Love/Blue Chameleon Ventures, 13 (bottom), 32
Charles W. Melton, cover, 11
Bob Miller, 14, 25, 34
Nature's Images/David T. Roberts, 26, 38
Unicorn Stock Photos/Marshall Prescott, 46
R.W. VanDevender, 22
Visuals Unlimited/William J. Weber, 6; Joe McDonald, 17, 43

2 3 4 5 6 05 04 03 02

Table of Contents

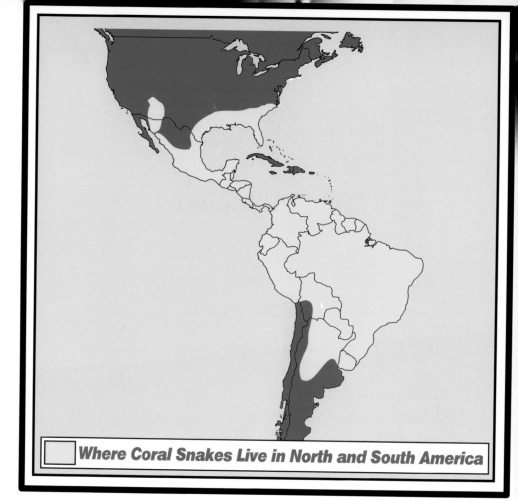

Where Coral Snakes Live in North and South America

Fast Facts about Coral Snakes

Kinds: There are more than 50 kinds of coral snakes in North and South America. Coral snakes are Elapids. Elapids have hollow teeth. Venom comes out of their teeth through small holes.

Description: Most coral snakes are two to four feet (61 to 122 centimeters) long. They are brightly colored with bands of red, yellow, and black.

Habits: Coral snakes often hide their heads under their bodies when they sense danger. They rarely bite humans.

Food: Most coral snakes eat small snakes. Some eat lizards and small animals like mice.

Reproduction: Different kinds of coral snakes mate at different times of the year. Female coral snakes lay two to 18 eggs after mating. The young coral snakes hatch after about two months.

Habitat: Coral snakes live in holes dug by small animals. They also live in logs, tree stumps, and piles of rotted leaves.

Range: Coral snakes live in the southern United States, Central America, and most of South America. Some coral snakes live in Asia.

Chapter 1

About Coral Snakes

Coral snakes are among the most deadly snakes in the world. Coral snakes got their name from North American explorers. The explorers thought the snakes looked like ocean coral. Ocean coral is a brightly colored group of underwater animals.

Coral snakes are members of the family Elapidae. A family is a group of animals with similar features. Elapids have hollow fangs. A fang is a long, sharp tooth. A fang has a hole

Explorers thought coral snakes looked like ocean coral.

at the end so venom can pass through it. Venom is a poisonous liquid produced by some animals.

Description

Many people think coral snakes are among the most beautiful snakes in the world. Most coral snakes have red, black, and yellow bands that wrap around their bodies. The red and yellow bands are right next to each other on U.S. coral snakes. The red and yellow bands of South American coral snakes are often separated by black bands.

Most coral snakes are two to four feet (61 to 122 centimeters) long. The longest coral snake ever found was more than five feet (more than 150 centimeters) long.

Most snakes have heads that are wider than their bodies. Coral snakes have small heads. Their heads are the same width as their bodies.

Coral snakes have small heads.

Where Coral Snakes Live

Coral snakes live in grasslands, in dry woods, and on rocky hillsides. Sometimes they live in ditches or along streams and riverbanks. Coral snakes usually avoid humans.

Many coral snakes live in holes dug by small animals. Some coral snakes live under rocks and logs. Most are nocturnal. Nocturnal means active at night.

Senses

Coral snakes sense mainly through smell and taste. They flick their forked tongues out every few seconds to smell and taste the air. Coral snakes rub their tongues against their Jacobson's organs. The Jacobson's organs are tiny sacs at the top of a snake's mouth. They are special taste and odor detectors.

Coral snakes cannot hear because they do not have eardrums. They do not have good vision, either. Coral snakes can only see objects that are very near.

Coral snakes molt two to 10 times each year.

Molting

Like all snakes, coral snakes molt. Molt means to shed an outer layer of skin. Coral snakes molt two to 10 times each year. Old coral snakes do not molt as often as young coral snakes.

A coral snake's colored bands turn pale before it molts. The outer layer of skin turns white as the snake sheds it. The snake slithers out of the old skin headfirst. The new skin is bright and colorful.

Coral Snake Look-Alikes

Most predators will not eat coral snakes. A predator is an animal that hunts and eats other animals. Some predators will not eat coral snake look-alikes either. Milk snakes and king snakes are two common coral snake look-alikes.

U.S. coral snakes have red and yellow bands next to each other. Look-alikes have red and black bands next to each other.

Another way to tell a coral snake from a look-alike is by its nose. Most coral snakes have black noses. Few look-alikes have black noses. Their noses are usually red or yellow.

Some people tell coral snakes from look-alikes by remembering a rhyme. The rhyme is:

Red against yellow, kill a fellow.
Red against black, poison lack.

Coral snake

U.S. coral snakes (above) have red and yellow
bands next to each other. Look-alikes (below)
have red and black bands next to each other.

King snake

Chapter 2

Hunting and Defense

Most coral snakes hunt and eat other snakes. Some eat other coral snakes. Others eat lizards and small animals.

Coral snakes rarely bite unless they are hunting. They hide their heads under their bodies if they sense danger. They will usually try to escape danger if they can.

Most coral snakes hunt at night.

Finding Prey

Most coral snakes hunt at night. Some coral snakes search under rocks and logs for prey. Prey is an animal hunted by another animal for food. Some coral snakes put their tails into animal holes. They shake their tails inside the holes to scare out prey. Other coral snakes hide under leaves or in cracked rocks. They wait for prey to come to them.

Coral snakes attack prey that comes near. They bite their prey and inject venom through their fangs. Coral snakes hold onto their prey and chew. They inject more venom while they are chewing.

Coral snakes often eat other small venomous snakes. They bite the other snakes near the head. They hold onto the snakes and try to keep from being bitten. Sometimes other snakes bite the coral snakes. Many coral snakes die from the bites of other snakes.

Some coral snakes wait for prey near rocks and logs.

Most coral snakes eat only small snakes.

Swallowing Food

The mouths of coral snakes are different than the mouths of most other snakes. Most other snakes can open their mouths wide to swallow large prey. Coral snakes cannot do this. They cannot eat prey larger than their own heads. That is why most coral snakes eat only small snakes.

A coral snake pulls prey into its mouth with its fangs. Most snakes eat their prey headfirst. But coral snakes sometimes swallow prey tailfirst. Coral snakes may take up to an hour to swallow prey.

Coral Snake Defenses

Some animals eat coral snakes. These animals are usually fast. They try to kill coral snakes quickly before the snakes can bite.

But most animals will not eat coral snakes. The red, black, and yellow bands tell predators that coral snakes are venomous. Most predators also avoid coral snake look-alikes.

Coral snakes flatten their bodies when predators attack them. Flattening their bodies makes coral snakes look bigger than they really are. This may scare predators away.

Some coral snakes bite predators that attack. They may try to inject the predators with venom. But coral snakes often do not use venom in defense.

Chapter 3

Coral Snake Venom

Coral snake venom is among the deadliest snake venoms in the world. A coral snake bite can kill a human if the bite is not treated. But few people die of coral snake bites. This is because coral snakes and people rarely encounter each other. Coral snakes are secretive creatures that usually come out only at night.

Coral snake fangs are small.

Coral snakes use their fangs on small prey.

Coral Snake Fangs

Coral snakes inject venom through their fangs. Their fangs are small. Coral snakes have difficulty biting objects larger than their heads. They use their fangs mostly on small prey.

Coral snakes control how much venom they release through their fangs. They use just a little venom when they bite small animals. They use more venom when they bite larger animals.

Sometimes coral snakes do not inject venom when they bite. These bites are called dry strikes. Dry strikes can occur when coral snakes bite to defend themselves.

Bite Victims

People can sometimes handle coral snakes without being bitten. But coral snake bites are dangerous when they do occur. Victims of coral snake bites may die quickly if they are not treated. Some victims die in less than a day.

Coral snakes' small fangs do not leave large wounds on their victims. Human victims may feel fine for several hours. Then they develop headaches and blurred vision. They have difficulty walking. Some have trouble breathing. Others lose feeling in parts of their bodies.

Treating Coral Snake Bites

The victim of a coral snake bite must see a doctor right away. Coral snake bites can be treated with an antivenin. An antivenin is a medicine that reduces the effects of venom. Scientists make antivenin from chemicals in snake venom.

Taking venom from a snake is dangerous. Scientists can take venom from large snakes like cobras and rattlesnakes easily. They hook the large snakes' fangs over a jar and let venom drip into it.

But a coral snake's mouth is much smaller. Scientists must put small tubes over a coral snake's fangs. They push up on the tubes to make the snake release venom. Scientists call this milking a snake.

Taking venom from a coral snake can be dangerous.

Chapter 4
Mating

Different kinds of coral snakes mate at different times of the year. Coral snakes do not stay together after mating. They do not take care of their young.

Approaching a Female

Mating is dangerous for a male coral snake. A male coral snake approaches a female to begin mating. He flicks his tongue against the female's body. This tells the female that the male is ready to mate.

Coral snakes do not stay together after mating.

Sometimes the female does not want to mate. The female may try to eat the male.

The female lifts her tail if she wants to mate. The male moves alongside her. Sometimes the female bites the male. But she does not inject venom. Scientists do not know why females do this. After the snakes have mated, the male slithers away.

Coral Snake Eggs

Female coral snakes lay eggs one to two months after mating. Females lay two to 18 eggs. The group of eggs is called a clutch. Females lay eggs in rotten logs, under rocks, and in small tunnels. They lay eggs in places where predators are unlikely to find them. They may lay eggs in more than one place.

Coral snake eggs are soft. Most eggs are white. Some are yellow. The eggs take one to two months to hatch.

Most coral snakes hatch from white eggs.

Young Coral Snakes

Coral snakes hatch by cracking their egg shells with a special tooth. Then they push their heads through the shells. Most coral snakes remain still after hatching. Some remain still for up to 12 hours. Scientists do not know why they do this.

Young coral snakes are paler than adults. They become more colorful after they molt for the first time. Most young coral snakes shed their skin about 20 days after they hatch.

Coral snakes are born with a supply of venom. They know how to hunt and swallow food. They also know how to avoid enemies.

Eggs in Ant Hills

Female Uruguayan (ur-uh-GWY-an) coral snakes lay eggs inside ant hills. Uruguayan

Young coral snakes become more colorful after they molt for the first time.

coral snakes live in northern South America. They slither into ant hills and lay eggs deep inside. They only lay eggs in hills built by a certain kind of ant.

The ants care for the coral snake eggs. They clean the eggs and keep other insects away from them. Coral snakes crawl out of the ant hills after they hatch. They usually stay near the ant hills. Coral snakes help the ants by eating other snakes in the area. Some of the other snakes would eat the ants if the coral snakes were not there.

Young coral snakes are born knowing how to hunt.

Chapter 5

Coral Snakes and People

People who are familiar with coral snakes know they should avoid being bitten. Some people call coral snakes 20-minute snakes. They believe that a coral snake's bite will kill a person in 20 minutes. This is not true. Most untreated victims live about a day after a bite occurs.

Some people call coral snakes 20-minute snakes.

Meeting a Coral Snake

Coral snakes rarely live in cities or near buildings. They usually come out at night. But sometimes coral snakes and people do meet.

Many people try to pick up coral snakes when they find them. They think the snakes are pretty. But picking up coral snakes is dangerous. The coral snake may bite if it senses danger. It is best to back away slowly if faced with a coral snake. The snake will usually try to escape.

People should also avoid coral snake look-alikes. Most coral snake look-alikes lack deadly venom. But some have venom that makes people sick. They may strike more readily than a coral snake.

The Coral Snake's Future

Some state governments once offered bounties on coral snakes. A bounty is money offered for

Coral snakes rarely live in cities or near buildings.

killing a venomous or harmful animal. Bounties led to many coral snake deaths. Few people hunt coral snakes today. Most people know that coral snakes will not harm them unless the snakes sense danger.

Some coral snakes have to move to new areas when people build cities near their homes. But coral snakes are not in danger of becoming extinct. Extinct means no longer living anywhere in the world.

Coral snakes are still among the most widespread snakes in North America and South America. They are also one of the most beautiful.

Coral snakes are among the most widespread snakes in North America and South America.

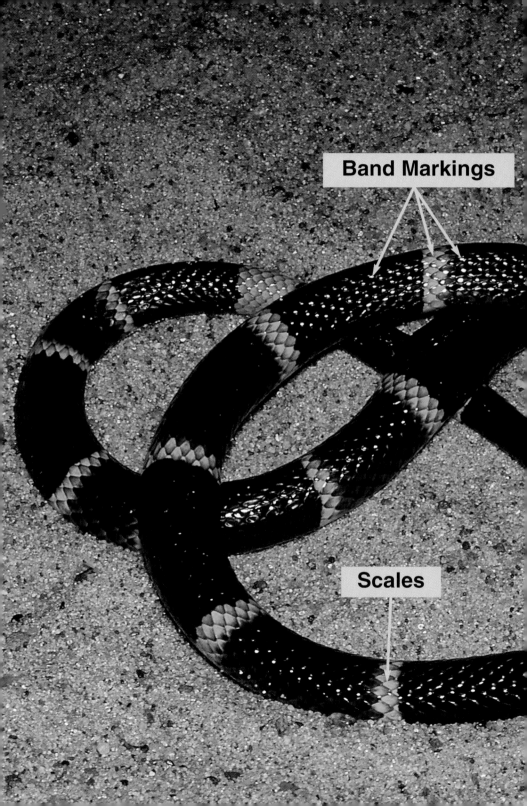

Band Markings

Scales

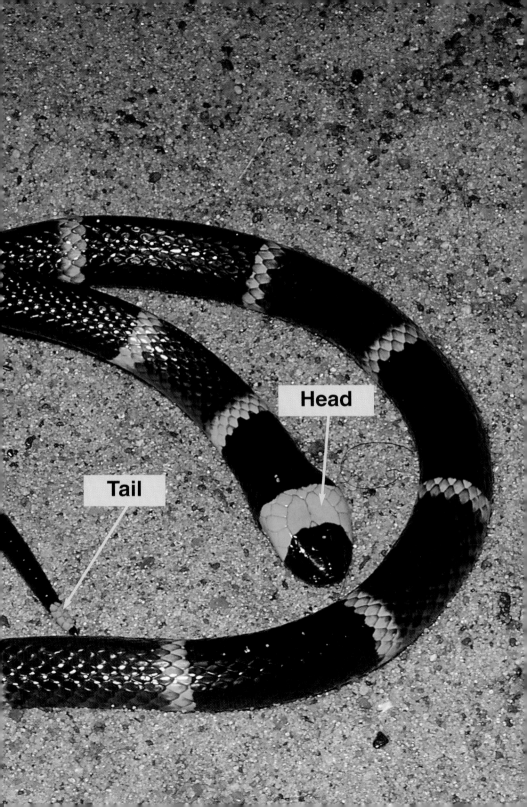

Head

Tail

Words to Know

antivenin (an-ti-VEN-in)—a medicine that reduces the effects of snake poison

bounty (BOUN-tee)—money offered for killing a venomous or harmful animal

clutch (KLUHCH)—a group of snake eggs

dry strike (DRYE STRIKE)—a venomless snake bite

extinct (ek-STINGKT)—no longer living anywhere in the world

fang (FANG)—a long, sharp tooth; venom passes through it.

molt (MOHLT)—to shed an outer layer of skin

nocturnal (nok-TUR-nuhl)—active at night

predator (PRED-uh-tur)—an animal that hunts and eats other animals

prey (PRAY)—an animal hunted by another animal for food

venom (VEN-uhm)—poison produced by some animals

To Learn More

Gerholdt, James E. *Snakes*. Edina, Minn.: Abdo & Daughters, 1994.

Grace, Eric S. *Snakes*. San Francisco: Sierra Club Books for Children, 1994.

Markle, Sandra. *Outside and Inside Snakes*. New York: Macmillan Books for Young Readers, 1995.

Stone, Lynn M. *Poison Fangs*. Vero Beach, Fla.: Rourke Press, 1996.

Useful Addresses

Metropolitan Toronto Zoo
Box 280
West Hill, Toronto
Ontario M1D 4R5
Canada

Miami Metrozoo
12400 Southwest 152nd Street
Miami, FL 33177

National Zoological Park
3001 Connecticut Avenue NW
Washington, DC 20008

**Society for the Study of Amphibians
    and Reptiles**
P.O. Box 626
Hays, KS 67601-0626

Internet Sites

**Bayou Bob's Brazos River
   Rattlesnake Ranch**
http://www.wf.net/~snake

The Belize Zoo—Coral Snake
http://belizezoo.org/zoo/zoo/herps/cor/
   cor1.html

Coral Snakes
http://www.tpwd.state.tx.us/adv/kidspage/
   snakes/psnakes.htm#3

Venomous Snakes
http://pelotes.jea.com/vensnake.htm

Index